TOUCHING OUR FAITH WITH EACH STEP

Our Pilgrimage Journey to the Holy Land

LORRIE BORCHERT, MA
ROB BORCHERT, MBA, MA

-PIECEWORK PUBLICATIONS

Copyright © 2018 by Lorrie Borchert

All rights reserved

> *No part of this book may be reproduced in any form or by any electronic or mechanical means, including information storage and retrieval systems, without written permission from the author, except for the use of brief quotations in a book review.*

ISBN 10 - 0999061364

ISBN 13 - 97809999061367

Cover Design by Sally Moore

❦ Created with Vellum

We dedicate this book to all those who have gone before us who helped impart the faith that we carry with us today.

Introduction

HOW THIS BOOK CAME ABOUT...

The actual writing of this book began just before I started to pack my suitcase for a Pilgrimage to the Holy Land.

I had been discussing places that had been on my bucket list and trips of a lifetime, as some people refer to them with friends and family for quite some time. These are trips that we would love to take someday, maybe....but we're not sure if they will ever really come about.

For us, we were lucky to meet the folks from Colette Travel and they suggested several different trips that we might consider taking with some of our local parishioners. Although many of them sounded exciting, the one that really sparked an interest for us was the trip to the Holy Land.

Very active in our parish, we had only dreamed about walking in the steps of our Lord in the land where it all happened! I know we weren't alone, as many people were interested in going along with us. However, it isn't always the right time due to financial restraints or health issues and so we had eight parishioners and ourselves.

Colette teamed us up with a parish from Hudson, Ohio that had two priests and 28 parishioners from their parish. Together we made a strong pilgrim team of forty.

They also provided us the most amazing tour guide. He was a local from Galilee and so he knew the area, the language and just where to take us.

His name was Read Makhouli and he has also written a book entitled: A Spiritual Journey: "Following the Footsteps of Jesus Christ our Lord. "

If we get to take another trip to the Holy Land, we will certainly ask for him to be our guide once again. His knowledge of ancient biblical history was outstanding and we all learned so much from him.

So, we invite you to come along with us on this

incredible faith-journey that we took in the fall of 2018. In this book wee have tried to paint a vivid description of what we saw and experienced so if you never get to go in person, we hope you get to sample a flavor of what we found while we were there.

We hope that we might have inspired you to think about taking a bucket list adventure such as this in your life - while you can.

A pilgrimage was an important trip for us, but maybe there is another kind of trip that might be important to you, one that you may have always wanted to do, but have never made the time or space in your life to make it come to life.

None of us know how much time we will be given, so make a plan and then work to make it happen. Try living your life without regrets!

Chapter One

"THE ANNOUNCEMENT" - NAZARETH

"And behold, you will conceive in your womb and bear a son, and you shall name Him, Jesus...The Holy Spirit will come upon you and the power of the Most High will overshadow you, and for that reason, the holy Child shall be called the Son of God." Luke 1:v31 and v35

Geographical Significance:

Nazareth is a small town (village) located about twenty miles southwest of the Sea of Galilee. It is a small village surrounded by other towns such as Nain, Cana, and Tiberias. There was quite a bit of trade and enterprise among these towns so that many occupations shared their talents with each other.

This is the village where Joachim and Anne, the parents of the Blessed Mother Mary, lived. It is also where Joseph, the foster father of Jesus went to live with Mary, his spouse. Although a small and inconspicuous village, it is the village where angels appeared and where Jesus was raised.

SCRIPTURAL SIGNIFICANCE:

Although this is the town of the Holy Family, the parents of Mary are not mentioned in the Bible. There are writings examined by the early Church fathers that tell the same story, that Mary was promised to Joachim and Anne by an angel, was consecrated to God and she remained a virgin all her life.

It is assumed that they were devotes Jews and were chosen in a special way to be part of our Salvation History. St. Joachim and St. Anne are the patron saints of grandparents.

Certainly, the other significant events in this small village was the appearance of the Angel Gabriel to the young girl, Mary, to tell her that she was to be the Mother of Our Savior, Jesus. And the fact that she said YES! Her YES brought about the beginning of our Salvation with the presence of Jesus here on earth.

The other Scriptural reference important to Nazareth is that it is the village that Jesus Christ grew up in. He went to the Synagogue there, he learned the Old Testament there, and He grew in Wisdom and Grace there.

∽

PERSONAL SIGNIFICANCE (ROB):

Having a strong devotion to Our Blessed Mother, our visit to Nazareth was very special. Being in the same village where Jesus grew up made me 'pause' in my footsteps to embrace the moment knowing that I was actually walking in the footsteps of Our Lord.

As part of this walk, we came to the Church of the Annunciation where we believe the church was built on the grounds of where the house of Mary was originally located.

This would make it the place where the Angel

Gabriel appeared to Mary to greet her and pose the angelic statement of Salvation.

Of course, Mary had to respond to this question and we all know the answer. Not just the 'YES" to the angel, but even more significant was her humility and obedience to God's Plan..."Be it done unto me according to Your Word"...(and the Word was made flesh).

Being in this (place) Church where Mary received a message from God, and even asked a question about the message, and then accepted God's Will, gave me both a historic and future experience.

Historic, because I thought about (and continue to think about) the times when a message comes to me from God (not an angel, but rather a 'situation') where I feel the situation is some kind of test or question involving a decision to move forward or not. In fact, I thought of this situation and that I even asked questions about it in order to "justify" moving forward. Taking a chance and saying YES, I moved forward and only (typically) in hindsight did I see the goodness of God in my life.

Interestingly enough, different situations went through my mind as we walked along and even today,

I get the same chilling sense of what my answer may be in order to move forward.

Today in these situations, I turn to Our Blessed Mother and ask her for guidance in making a decision that will praise her Son. I have great confidence that she will not steer me down the wrong path.

Snippets (Lorrie):

I stood on a long line (with many other pilgrims) waiting to view what had been Mary's house. It was now a grotto situated within the Basilica of the Annunciation, located in the town of Nazareth.

The front of what they refer to as "Mary's House" was enlarged and open to the public and revealed a simple altar. A long, black wrought iron fence separated the pilgrims from the actual house. Behind the altar we could see some simple stairs leading to an upstairs room.

As we stood on the level above the house, we could view the side of the house that appeared to be made of cement blocks. The house backed up into dirt, as a cave would.

It was a quick glimpse of what the home of Mary must have been like. Was she sitting in this space when the angel appeared to her?

From the elevated area I stood and prayed the Joyful decade of the rosary and tried to take in the significance of where I was so I could always remember this very moment when I would say this particular rosary in the future.

Chapter Two

"THE NATIVITY" - BETHLEHEM

"Glory to God in the highest and on earth; Peace among men with whom He is pleased." Luke 2: v7 and v14

Geographic Significance:

The location of the city of David, Bethlehem, is significant in itself as it is about five miles south of Jerusalem. Many travelers to and from Jerusalem found a place to stay in Bethlehem.

Another key geographic significance is that Mary and Joseph had to travel from Nazareth to Bethlehem since Joseph was in the line of David…a distance of seventy plus miles. It was a city with much activity since it acted like a suburb of Jerusalem and there were many tradesmen who had animals to trade and to livery and everyone wanted to be involved with the exchange of goods.

Since David was a young King, there were many people present for the census since his family members were vast.

Scriptural Significance:

Bethlehem, the City of David (because David was born here), has ancient names associated with it. Some know the city as Ephrata, some as the Shepherd's Field, as well as the Field of Boaz. According to the Old Testament, in Samuel, it is the city where David was anointed by the man of God, Samuel as king over Israel.

So what does, Bethlehem mean?

In Hebrew, the first part of the name means "house" and the last part means "bread"; so together, it is called the House of Bread. How significant the name change, as it is the birthplace of our Bread of Life, the Lord Jesus.

The prophet Micah foretells the birth of Jesus in Chapter 4, v8..

"And you tower of the flock, hill of the daughter of Zion, to you it shall come, the former dominion shall come."

And in Chapter 5: v 2-3,

> *"But you, O Bethlehem of Ephrata, who are one of the little clans of Judah, from you shall come forth for me one who is to rule in Israel, whose origin is from old, from ancient days. Therefore he shall give them up until the time when she who is in labor has brought fourth; then the rest of his kindred shall return to the people of Israel."*

Bethlehem, the city where the universal message of the New Covenant was presented in the form of an infant, is the universal message to the lonely and poor of the world (represented by the Shepherds) and to the many nations around the world (represented by the Wise Men) of the great love that God has for us in sending His Son.

Personal Significance (Rob)

Before entering the Church of the Nativity, our tour guide took us to the "Shepherds' Field" where it is said that the angels appeared to the shepherds to announce the birth of Jesus. This field is full of caves and have been used as natural stables to keep the sheep and goats for centuries.

We went into one of these caves and here there was a small 'altar' and writings on the walls. We gathered round and sat where we could while one of our priests talked about the 'place' we were at. Here was the first announcement of God's great gift to us; here was the first sign (in that of the angels appearance) that God was intervening into our lives; here was the first opportunity for us, as mankind, to respond to God's message in our lives. We had a moment of silence and then broke into song (Christmas Carols) smiling and joyful to be where we were.

We then proceeded to the Church of the Nativity which is a beautiful church filled with wonderful displays of God in our lives and of Mary and Joseph and their special place in our Salvation History.

Chapter 2

Within this church was the entrance into what is stated to be the actual birthplace of Our Lord. The entrance was very small and one had to bend over and squat to enter into this place.

With all of the pilgrims there, one can only picture the crowd and the pushing. However, there was an excitement and a peace about where we were.

As I grew closer to the "spot," I could see a designated star above the declared birth location. I knelt down before this area and was able to put my head into the opening and kiss the birth spot where Our Lord was born.

What a thrill and chill to be filled with that grace! As I stood, they pointed to the other side and said that this is where the manger was placed for the Baby Jesus. I was able to touch this spot also and then we went back up to the formal Church.

We were going to celebrate Mass at this Church and I was vesting as Deacon. I was also given the honor and privilege to preach and give the homily during this Mass. What an immense sensation of grace to share with others the beginnings of New Testament Salvation History.

While standing in one of the 'cave' chapels, my

heart was filled with joy realizing that I was in the same 'space' as the infant Jesus and Mary and Joseph. I felt as if that joy and grace was beaming out to all present as I gave my homily. Tears came to my eyes as I expressed my faith and felt the fullness of God's presence with all of us. It was a Mass and a moment that I will never forget.

Snippets (Lorrie):

The door was small and for the entrance into a church we though it very unusual. I watched six foot plus men having to fold themselves in half to enter. Later we were told it was built this way to keep the invaders out.

And so we entered the Church of the Nativity. We got onto the end of a very long line and after waiting for an hour or two, we finally came to the stairs down into what had been the original site of the birth of Jesus.

It was a very small room, reminiscent of a cave, but there were many people crammed into this small space and very little time to take it all in. A loud voice kept reminding us to "Move along," in

Chapter 2

an attempt to keep the traffic moving in and out of the space.

Suddenly I saw what appeared to be a gold star on the floor and people were bending down to touch it. I followed suit and put my hand on the star. Then I stood up and looked to my left and saw people touching the area where the manger was thought to be placed. With a very quick touch, I placed my hand on it as I was being swept along to the exit.

It took a moment or two to register the fact that I had just touched the place where our Lord was born. We did not, however, have too much time for reflection, because we needed to make our way to a tiny, out of the way chapel where our tour group was scheduled to have mass.

The room was hewn out of rock and painted white. It had a simple altar and a number of benches placed around the room. Our two priests celebrated mass for our group and Deacon Rob got to preach the homily.

Knowing how he is drawn to Our Lady, I was not surprised that he asked to preach at this important site where our salvation history began. He seemed to stand in awe and was transfixed with the significance of the space.

This was a special moment we won't soon forget but will take with us always.

Chapter Three

"THE FORERUNNER OF JESUS" - EIN KAREM

"And you, my child, will be called the prophet of the Most High; for you will go on BEFORE THE LORD AND PREPARE HIS WAY; to give His people the knowledge of salvation by the forgiveness of their sins." Luke 1: v75 and v77

Geographical Significance:

Although no one actually knows where Jesus was baptized except that it was in the Jordan River, Ein Karem is a small spot northeast of Bethany and it is in this region that Jesus was baptized by John the Baptist.

The exact spot on the Jordan is really not the vital reason for us to celebrate the Baptism of Jesus, the vital reason is that it was a place where the river did not have a fast current and a place where a person of reasonable height could stand up. There are a few spots like this so the people chose one and established it as a "special place" where other Baptisms could occur.

SCRIPTURAL SIGNIFICANCE:

The Scriptural reference above is actually the reference from Zachariah's prayer at the birth of his son, John the Baptist.

If you recall, Zachariah was made speechless after receiving the message from the angel that his wife, Elizabeth, would become pregnant and bear a son whose name would be John. Since Elizabeth was the cousin of Mary, the Blessed Mother, this would make John and Jesus cousins as well.

The connection for me is that when Jesus entered into the presence of the unborn child John, the unborn child leapt "for joy" in the womb of Elizabeth.

Now, at the Jordan, John openly declares Jesus as the Messiah and that Jesus should baptize him. This is also where John publicly declares, in a loud voice, "Behold the Lamb of God!"

John was truly the forerunner of Jesus in that he prepared the people to recognize within themselves how they have sinned against God in many ways. John was declaring that people needed to recognize their sins and ask for forgiveness. John further stated that he only baptized with water but that someone was coming (Jesus) who would baptize with both water and the Holy Spirit.

Personal Significance:

The Jordan experience was one where you had to take yourself out of the present situation and strive to physically take yourself back to the days of Jesus and John the Baptist. In trying to do this myself, I was picturing the time of John and the crowd of people standing on the shore listening to him preach about the Kingdom and then entering into the water to be baptized.

When you arrive at this "place," there are lots of men

and women's lockers where you can place your clothes and then put on a white garment (over your bathing suit). All those from our group who wanted the experience did just this.

I led those from our group to a specific and "not-crowded" area of the River Jordan and entered into the water. It was a little chilly, but the first two people into the water were myself and one of the priests from Ohio. He re- baptized* me and I re-baptized* him. It was a wonderful and physical experience to feel the water all over your body and he placed my head in the Jordan and pronounced the words of Baptism. (*Note: This re-baptism was strictly a reenactment of our original baptism since we had already been baptized in our catholic faith).

Once I was re-baptized*, I invited all from our group to come into the water for their own individual experience in the River Jordan. It was wonderful and joyful and everyone was laughing in a spiritual manner.

There was great joy among our entire tour group and one could feel the freedom of the Lord's grace flowing both in the water and as we got out of the water. We did stay for a short time in the water as more people were coming to our spot.

The beauty of this experience was enhanced when a person, (not from our group), came over and asked Father if he would baptize him and he did. We don't know if the man knew what Baptism truly involves but the actual Sacrament took place within our group. Praise God!

∾

SNIPPETS: (Lorrie)

The bus stopped at a spot where baptisms were being performed. Upon inspecting the site, we saw men, women and children dressed in white garments over their bathing suits.

We were led into the gift shop where we could each rent a white garment, if we wished to be re-baptized* in the River Jordan.

Although I had been baptized years ago, I wanted to have the experience of being symbolically baptized in the same water where John the Baptist performed this for our Lord and make a recommitment to my original baptism made 46 years ago when I began a catholic at age 21.

As I made my way down the mossy steps into the murky river, I tred slowly and carefully, not knowing what was underfoot or how deep the water would be. I noticed there were different sections marked off by a string of white buoy's so that bathers could not venture into the deeper sections of the river.

I stood quietly as I saw our priest John, re-baptize* Deacon Rob and then he, in turn, re-baptized* Father John. I was next and although the water was cold and dark, I found it refreshing in both sensation and spiritually.

I tried to take in the significance of standing in the river Jordan and being baptized as Jesus was. A moment to remember, for sure!

Once finished, I made my way back to the chaos of the bath house where women of every size and nationality were getting dressed. Most had smiles on their faces and seemed very kind and approachable all of us touched by the mutual experience we had just shared.

Chapter 4

"THE MARRIAGE FEAST OF CANA" - CANA

"Do whatever He tells you." John 2: v5

Geographical Significance:

Cana is a small village, about 3 or 4 miles north of Nazareth. It is a village filled with connected families who all worked together and played together.

Cana is popular today as many people go there to experience the place where the first miracle of Jesus occurred and to renew their own wedding vows.

Today, of course, it has grown into the size of a small city, but the attraction to visit and renew your wedding vows is still there.

Scriptural Significance:

We all know the scriptural significance of this small village of Cana. In fact, in the time of Jesus, Cana was a small village that probably contained some relatives of Joseph and Mary who invited them to the wedding.

In those days, weddings lasted for about a week at the home of the new bride and groom. With that, you can imagine that after three days (when Jesus and Mary and the disciples arrived), that the wine was gone.

Although it appeared strange for Jesus to respond to His Mother in the way that He did, she had all of the confidence and trust in Him that she told the waiters to "do whatever He tells you"...and they did. Thus, the best wine and the first miracle.

Another scriptural significance is that here, in Cana, Jesus turned water into wine; at the Last

Supper, Jesus turned wine into His blood; and on the Cross, both blood and water came forth from the side of Jesus when pierced by the soldier.

Personal Significance (Rob):

The first miracle of Cana, besides the changing of water into wine, is also our Church's theological approach to the Sacrament of Matrimony.

Remember that a Sacrament is an outward sign instituted by Jesus to give grace. The couple is the outward sign; instituted by Christ and is the calling of the two people together to live a life dedicated to each other; and to give grace is the caring that they have for one another is the giving of their total selves to each other.

The changing of the water into wine symbolizes the changing of the personal single identity to the identity of a couple.

At Cana, we were able to celebrate Mass and at this Mass, I stayed with my wife, Lorrie, so that we could renew our wedding vows.

This Mass was extremely significant as it

incorporated the miracle of the changing of the water into wine, but also reminded me (us) of the changing of ourselves into a dedicated love for each other and the true gift that God has given me.

After Mass, we had some time to shop and we bought ourselves some Cana wine and two new wedding rings to celebrate. There is writing on the rings in Hebrew that says "this is the gift of love from me to you." A very special stop during our journey with Jesus.

Snippets (Lorrie):

Yes, the ability to renew our marriage vows where Jesus performed his first miracle was amazing and very special!

We stood in the pews and followed along with the mass until it was time for us to join hands with our beloved and renew our marriage vows. For us, we had originally said those vows 47 years ago, but my voice quivered exactly as it had all those many years ago and ironically, exactly in the same places! As I gazed around the church, I could see the other couples with tears streaming down their cheeks as well. This was definitely a high point of our trip and one that we would always remember.

We had read in the Bible about the big stone water jars that held the water for the guests at the wedding that Jesus and his mother attended.

As we descended the stairs to the basement of the church, we found ourselves in a hewed out area with one very large stone jar.

In my head I'd always thought that it might have been made out of terra-cotta, but I saw that it was very large and made out of pebbles and concrete and appreciated that it could hold 50+ gallons of water. This was what Jesus turned from water into wine!

There were some benches that lined the walls of this small space and a clear plastic barrier was erected on the top of the hollowed out wall. I saw a man throw a small piece of paper behind the clear plastic. Upon closer inspection I could see many small notes in a pile behind the plastic.

So I sat down on a bench and tore out a page from my field journal and grabbed a pen and wrote out my own small note of prayer to cast up with the others. It was a small plea to keep our marriage alive and strong and to follow His will for our lives. What better place to leave a prayer such as this?

The rest of the group seemed to be gathered around the bottom of the stairs where one of our fellow pilgrims from Ohio had slipped and had hurt her leg on the stairs. Later we learned that she had broken her leg and would need to fly home. Her friends carried her out to the bus where they quizzed our tour guide about ER's and Clinic's. We took her back to the hotel and they made some phone calls.

I neglected to say that we actually made two stops to Cana. The first time we stopped there we were 5 minutes too late and the gate was closed.

Our guide tried to reach the Sister in charge and while all of this negotiation was going on, I slipped into the Cana wine shop across the way and sipped some Cana wine.

The upshot was that I got separated from the group. They all went on to the bus and I found myself all alone without any information about my bus number, driver's name or hotel name. I got very scared indeed! A small, still voice inside said, "do not be afraid," and so when several men approached me asking me if I was lost and told me not to be afraid, I followed them to where the tour buses normally parked and found my tour bus and was reunited with my group. It could have gone terribly wrong (I know) and I should have kept that important information on my person and the the ear piece plugged into my ear.

Lessons learned! Truly, it was an experience of being the lost sheep!

Chapter 5

"WALKING ON THE WATER" - THE SEA OF GALILEE

"When the disciples saw Him walking on the sea, they were terrified and said "It is a ghost!" and they cried out in fear. But immediately Jesus spoke to them saying, "Take courage, it is I; do not be afraid, Come...You of little faith, why did you doubt?" Matt 14: v26 and 27; v29 and v31

∼

Geographic Significance:

The Sea of Galilee is located 80 miles north of Jerusalem and 20 miles northeast of Nazareth. There were many fishermen who fished every day for their living. The Sea of Galilee measures 13 miles in length, 7.5 miles wide and about 150 feet deep. It's circumference measures about 34 miles around and receives an average of 150 inches of rain per year.

A popular fish from this sea is "St. Peter's fish" which is a tropical fish (tilapia) that breeds and multiplies only in shallow waters. Another fact is that this fish can only be fished and caught at night. (Remember, St. Peter was fishing all night long and caught nothing when Jesus told him to go fishing deep and during the day). Peter listened to the Lord caught so many fish that his boat was almost sank.

∽

SCRIPTURAL SIGNIFICANCE:

The name of the Sea of Galilee is mentioned in the Gospels of Matthew and Mark. Luke calls it "the Lake" and "The Lake of Gennesaret". The Gospel of John calls it the "Sea of Tiberias, named after the Caesar of Rome, Tiberius. It plays a role in our Scriptural heritage in that it 'provides a stage' upon which the goodness, the power and the majesty of Jesus comes forth very clearly.

In Mark 4, there is the sudden storm on the Sea that occurs as the Apostles (with Jesus) are trying to cross over to the other side. From this story, we should learn that this sea resembles our own life and that sometimes (and suddenly) we have those high waves, the times of hardship and afflictions. We should also learn that we should always call upon Jesus Christ and turn these burdens and hardships over to Him in total trust because He is the Almighty.

The St. Peter's fish we have already mentioned above in the geographical section and that total trust expressed by Peter shows us how Jesus' love and concern for our wellbeing is always there… and given back a hundredfold.

~

Personal Significance (Rob):

Being on a boat on the Sea of Galilee was a wonderful experience in realizing what a hard life the Apostles, who were fishermen, lived.

They had to have a tough spirit and determination in doing this task every day. In fact, it wasn't a task, it was a matter of survival! Yes, you could catch fish and have a meal for a day but you needed to catch a lot of fish to feed your family and to store some away in case you did not catch any for a day or two or more.

I began to realize that Jesus' first choice were men

who were determined, who had a purpose in their life, and who knew what it meant to struggle and to survive?

I thought of my own life and what this means to me. Am I determined? How do I handle my struggles? How do I care for myself and others? What I did realize is that these first few chosen men made it through life and then...by following Jesus, to put their total trust in Him and in God to continue to take care of their families and themselves.

They did not think of themselves anymore but of how important it was to take care of others. The boat was a resting place to contemplate these things.

Then I looked around and saw the small villages and towns on the mountainside all around the Sea of Galilee and how peaceful it all looked.

I thought of the storms on the Sea that are described in the Bible and I asked one of the crew if storms came up on the Sea and he told me that they did indeed and many times without any warning. I thought of the Bible stories of the Apostles and Jesus in the boat when a storm suddenly came up and how afraid they were while Jesus peacefully slept through it. They woke Him up and asked for help. Jesus saw their fear and told them not to be afraid but to trust in Him. He then silenced the wind and calmed the Sea and they were "amazed".

The other prominent story is about the Apostles in the boat in another storm and Jesus comes to them walking on the water. They could not believe it and thought that He was a ghost and when they realized that it was Jesus, Peter asked to come to Him and He told Peter "Come."

Peter did and then realized the power of the storm and started to sink. Jesus picked him up and they both went into the boat where He said to them...Oh, ye of little faith!

While still on the boat and later on the bus ride, I had to examine my level of trust and faith in Jesus. Sure, I am a deacon but trust and faith are always a personal matter whether you are ordained or not. Trust – in turning everything over to the Lord and that He will take care of me and my needs. How much do I do myself and not depend on the Lord? How often do I take on a project, help someone, visit someone and 'take the credit,' which is why it all turned out well?

Did I miss the fact that Jesus was very present in each circumstance? Did I pray for assistance beforehand? Did I thank Him afterwards? Do I have more trust in myself or in Him? This also seems to tie right into how strong is my faith!

Faith and trust appear to be very contingent on each other, as least for me. Do I have enough faith and trust to step out of the boat and walk (or follow) Jesus?

Do I have enough faith and trust to know that He will catch me if I begin to drown in my lack of faith and lack of trust?

What do I have to do to enhance my faith and trust in Him?

These are questions and actions that I must continually ask myself.

SNIPPETS (LORRIE):

The bus stopped and we walked, single file toward the Sea of Galilee before us. We boarded a large wooden boat and sat on benches that lined each side of the length of the boat. It was made of dark brown wood and had the rigging for a sail, but we motored out into the lake quietly and without fuss and listened to our guide point to the sites along the shore.

We saw the hill where the 5,000 were fed and could only imagine what it must have felt like to be in the crowd on that day sitting on the hill as Jesus was in a small boat down below.

Further along the shore we saw the place where the Beatitudes were given. Later we were walking on the grounds of this site, we could look down toward the water and imagine Jesus walking on the water and his disciples pulling fish into the nets after fishing for hours without any luck.

We sailed past all of these sites with a gentle breeze blowing over the lake and perfect temperatures making the whole experience one to remember. The water had no waves and had a green cast to it. Unlike the salty Dead Sea, this was filled with fresh water.

After the boat ride we would visit each of these sites and learn in depth what happened. the Bible stories once memorized in Sunday school came to life when you stood on the spot and looked out over the Sea of Galilee and realized that the story and your faith had met and you were actually standing in the place that you had only previously read or heard about.

Chapter 6

"MULTIPLICATION OF THE LOAVES AND FISHES" - TABGHA

"There is a lad here who has five barley loaves and two fish, but what are these for so many people?"...."When they were filled, He said to His disciples, Gather up the leftover fragments so that nothing will be lost. So they gathered them up and filled twelve baskets with fragments from the five barley loaves which were left over by those who had eaten." John 6: v9 and v13

Geographic Significance:

Tabgha is an area southwest of Capernaum. It is off of the Sea of Galilee and has the Mount of the Beatitudes as its western vision backdrop. It is an open area where lots of boats (in Jesus' time) could be moored as part of a fishing village. In this area, a basilica was built around 480 A.D. in recognition of this feeding of the multitude. The stone under the altar is said to be where Jesus stood and blessed the food. The basilica was destroyed in 614 A.D. by the Persians and was left "buried" until 1932 when two German Benedictine monks discovered it while excavating. In 1995, a new church was built in the same style, the same size and design as the old Byzantine basilica as these monks found and preserved an icon which depicted the original model. The inside of this basilica is full of mosaics and under the altar, the stone is still present and in front of the altar is a mosaic which depicts the loaves and fish that feed the multitude.

~

Scriptural Significance:

This scriptural scene takes place by the side of the Sea of Galilee. Jesus, say a week or two before, sent out the seventy-two (two by two) and His own Apostles to share the "Good News" and preach the Gospel. He gave the seventy-two a command to bring the Word of God and His message of forgiveness and love to as much geography as possible.

He gave His Apostles the same message to share but He also told them not to take anything with them, such as food or clothing, and to totally depend on God.

Here, while Jesus was at the shore of the Sea, He saw them all return and how excited they were in spreading the "Good News". He also saw how tired they were from their journeys.

He told them to sit down and rest and then asked His Apostles what was there to feed these people. His Apostles were amazed at what He asked and told Him that the only food around was what some young boy had from fishing in the Sea and the bread that his mother gave him to eat.

We know the rest of the story. The power of His great love and caring multiplied these loaves and fishes to not only feed the thousands who were there but also have food left over.

This miracle points out that with faith, something very small and insignificant can become a continuing moment of grace in many lives.

PERSONAL SIGNIFICANCE:

This was a very beautiful and peaceful spot. The church was a place where you have to imagine Jesus present and with His Twelve Apostles. The mosaic floors were magnificent and meaningful when you took the time to appreciate the scenery. The view outside was also magnificent and one could picture the thousands of people milling around and talking about their own experiences.

You could also imagine the 'thirst' of these people for more teachings from Jesus. Their yearning could not be satisfied but Jesus knew that their hunger could be satisfied. Jesus always knows what we need and gives it to us generously...we don't even have to ask.

As a deacon, looking out at the congregation at each Mass I can see in many this same hunger for more teachings from Jesus. I see all of the people at each Mass with different expressions and different ways of experiencing what they are hearing and how they are participating. From young to old, they are all searching for some experience with God and with Jesus.

This is why reading the scriptures with expression is

so important. This is why reading the Gospel and presenting a 'Spirit-filled' homily is so important. I am not saying that I am a good homilist, but I now have more awareness of the various needs of the parish.

I have also discovered that each of our Masses has a different personality and have determined that each personality should be treated differently.

I, too, search for meaning in the scriptural readings and read them over the night before. This is not because I am a deacon, it is because I am searching for ways to get closer to Jesus in each of the readings and in the music.

I pray that you, too, willcontinue to search for Jesus in any way you find helpful and satisfying.

Snippets (Lorrie):

We have heard this bible story so many times as we have grown up it in our faith. We wondered just how it was possible to turn this small amount of food into enough food to feed so many?

Truly it was a miracle to behold and I am sure that many who experienced this food were touched in a way that they never forgot.

How many times have we experienced this expansion story in our own lives? As a Mom of six, I often would go and check out the pantry and wonder how I would be able to find enough food to feed my hungry family. We had some ongoing medical problems with one of our children that severely challenged our financial security and so many times I have had the opportunity to see meagre resources stretched beyond what I could have imagined and I think back to this story in the Bible and smile.

This is an ongoing kind of miracle that continues to happen in our lives when we invite guests to come over after church for lunch (as an example) not knowing if there will be enough food to feed them, but trusting that the Lord will provide and help me stretch the little I may have into just enough so that all may be fed.

I never thought that I would be able to travel to this place and experience it for myself! It was really a blessing to do so!

Chapter 7

"THE SERMON ON THE MOUNT"

"Blessed are..." The Beatitudes - (Matthew 5:1:12)

"Blessed are the poor in spirit..."

"Blessed are the meek..."

"Blessed are those who mourn..."

The Beatitudes, Matthew 5: 1:12

GEOGRAPHIC SIGNIFICANCE:

The traditional location for the Mount of Beatitudes is on the northwestern shore of the Sea of Galilee.

The formation of the Mount is in the shape of a natural theater and has a very unique natural acoustic system.

In fact, this natural acoustic system has been tested by many and what they found was that if one stood at the top of the Mount and projected their voice, it could be heard at the bottom of the Mount and vice versa. The quality of the voice (sound) in either direction was excellent and indicates that one could make a 'presentation' here very successfully.

SCRIPTURAL SIGNIFICANCE:

The fullness of the Beatitudes is found in Matthew's Gospel. Matthew wrote his Gospel to the Jewish people and therefore many of the stories and events are relational to the Old Testament and the Jewish faith. Matthew wanted to show (in writing) that Jesus was the fulfillment of the Old Testament and therefore the Messiah.

The 'Sermon on the Mount" is relational to Moses receiving the Ten Commandments on Mount Sinai. As Moses delivered the Ten Commandments to the Jewish people from Mount Sinai, Jesus delivered the new law from the Mount of Beatitudes.

The Ten Commandments were inter-relational as the first three were directed with the relationship with God and the next seven directed the relationship mankind.

The Beatitudes are also inter-relational since one cannot be a 'peacemaker' if one is not 'meek in the heart'. The inter-connection of the Beatitudes is experienced within each one.

∾

PERSONAL SIGNIFICANCE:

Looking down from the Mount of the Beatitudes was a beautiful site. As one can imagine, it was a fairly clear area for many people (at that time) to sit and share with each other.

Following Jesus, at that time, was an adventure in that you really did not know where you were going or what to expect. Listening to Jesus' words had to be a very focusing experience since you did not want to miss a thing.

Looking out into the area, I actually felt a 'silence' and could imagine hearing these words from Jesus. Realizing the wonderful acoustics of this place, the silence of the crowd had to be a holy experience in itself. Then, hearing the words "Blessed are...." one can only imagine what was going through the minds of the people as to comparing themselves, or not, to one of the beatitudes.

The Church of the Beatitudes was unique also in that unlike the standard church with the interior being in the formation of a cross, this Church was circular.

We walked around the altar in a circular pattern and while praying in one spot, I realized the circular, inter-relational aspects of the Beatitudes themselves.

These new statements or guidance challenged me (and you) to live in a new light. These statements may appear to be general, but they are actually very specific offer guidance for every situation.

I also realized that, for me at least, these Beatitudes can be great for an 'examination of conscience' before the Sacrament of Reconciliation. When we live by them, we are truly blessed and so are everyone around us.

SNIPPETS (LORRIE):

I stood with my arms outstretched from the walkway overlooking the Sea of Galilee. I stood thinking about how important the Beatitudes are for me in my daily life, and for other as well.

As I stood there, I imagined Jesus gently giving these words to the audience gathered around to hear them. As we listened to our guide, I imagined how people came from a distance to hear Jesus. The acoustics from this place are wonderful, so I imagined that His voice would be carried on the wind. The spot where we sat was on a hill overlooking the Sea of Galilee.

The grounds of this church and space were very lush with vegetation and beautiful flowers.

Once inside the church, we walked around the inside, trying to take it all in. There were many pilgrims who were visiting this spot on the day that we were there. Many tour buses were in the parking lot and it was a time to pay attention, so we would not get separated from our group or get on the wrong numbered bus.

Chapter 8

"THE TEACHING PLACE OF JESUS" - CAPERNAUM

"So when the crowd saw that Jesus was not there, nor his disciples, they themselves got into the small boats and came to Capernaum seeking Jesus...Then they said to Him, Lord always give us this bread. Jesus said to them, 'I am the bread of life; he who comes to Me will not hunger, and he who believes in Me will never thirst." John 6: v 25; v34 and v35

∼

Geographic Significance:

Capernaum is a fishing village on the northwestern

shore of the Sea of Galilee. It was the center of Jesus' Galilean ministry.

Capernaum is the first town on the lakeshore inside the realm of Antipas as one came from Bethsaida, which lay inside the territory of the tetrarch Philip. Capernaum was a very active town of travelers as they came west from Bethsaida, south from Caesarea Philippi and north from Tiberias and even by boat from the south.

S̲c̲r̲i̲p̲t̲u̲r̲a̲l̲ ̲S̲i̲g̲n̲i̲f̲i̲c̲a̲n̲c̲e̲:

From a scriptural sense, Capernaum is well known since it is the place that we believe Jesus stayed for a long time during His ministry.

This is the town where Jesus preached in the synagogue and commanded many evil spirits to come out of people.

He also went and stayed with Peter in his house (for three years according to St. Luke's Gospel) where He cured Peter's mother-in-law and cured the man who was lowered from the roof top since there was no room in the house.

Remnants of the house of St. Peter is still there You can see the various rooms and, in a sense, how they lived.

It is from here that, we believe, Jesus went out into the other surrounding areas and preached and cured people, but then returned to Capernaum. This is well known town in the Scriptures.

~

Personal Significance:

Walking along the streets of Capernaum and realizing that Jesus walked these same pathways, I received a sense of peace and wonderment.

When we stopped, I asked myself if I was standing in a spot where Jesus cured someone or cast out an evil spirit?

I kept asking myself this same question throughout our stay at Capernaum and also tried to picture where Jesus would have sat or slept in Peter's house.

It was a personal experience for me being surrounded by the awe that Jesus lived, loved, prayed and cured in this town and specifically in this area around Peter's house.

Yes, there was the busyness of the city and yes there were many people moving about including our tour but, for me, there was a peace and serenity.

I felt peace in knowing that the power of Jesus was thread throughout these buildings and especially at the remains of the house of St. Peter. I felt serenity in knowing that the grace of the Holy Spirit was ever present and that not only I but the whole tour group was being filled with this grace as we "lived where Jesus lived."

Capernaum required focus due to the many distractions but once you focused, this grace filled you and you felt the warmth of the presence of God.

Sharing a meal at a Jewish community, known as a kibbutz, was a wonderful experience and reminder of how wonderful communal life can be when you turn your life over to God and trust totally in Him.

I prayed that this wonderful sense of community, peace and grace would continue in my life after we returned home. Thus far, it comes and goes but when I am with my family and my parish family, the sense of Jesus' presence brings back all of those feelings.

SNIPPETS (LORRIE):

Once we finished our our boat ride on the Sea of Galilee we were able to visit the site of where it was thought that Peter's house was located during the time of Jesus.

We were told that he had spent time here, in this spot and also taught in the local synagogue.

He preached here and performed many healing miracles, including the healing of Simon's mother-in-law from a fever.

Our group visited the remains of the synagogue that had been built in the 3rd century AD on the site of the one that stood here in Jesus's day.

The black basalt blocks forming the foundations of the earlier synagogue built by a Roman centurion (see Luke 7:5) could be clearly seen.

Now a modern Franciscan church – in the shape of a boat – it was built in 1990 over the remains of a house believed to be the home of Simon Peter – where Jesus healed Peter's mother-in-law. The original house had been converted into an octagonal church in the 5th century.

Chapter 9

"THE TRANSFIGURATION" - MOUNT TABOR

"And He was transfigured before them; and His face shone like the sun and His garments became as white as light. And behold Moses and Elijah appeared to them, talking with Him. Peter said to Jesus, 'Lord, it is good for us to be here...'"Matthew 17: v2, 3, and 4

Geographical Significance:

Mount Tabor is shaped almost like a half sphere suddenly rising from rather flat surroundings and reaching a height of 1,886 feet.

The Catholic church, called the Church of the Transfiguration, at the top is very visible from afar.

At its base it is almost fully surrounded by the Arab villages of Daburiyya, Shibli, and Umm al-Ghanam. is located in Lower Galilee, Israel, at the eastern end of the Jezreel Valley, 11 miles west of the Sea of Galilee.

It is believed by many Christians to be the site of the Transfiguration of Jesus. Mount Tabor is known as Itabyrium in the Graeco-Roman world, and the Mount of Transfiguration in some Christian contexts.

∽

SCRIPTURAL SIGNIFICANCE:

If you see a picture of Mount Tabor, it stands out amid the surrounding area and rises above the plain.

According to the Scripture, Jesus left the disciples at the foot of the Mount and took Peter, James and John up the Mount. When they reach the top, Jesus was transfigured from the human side to the divine side and Moses and Elijah also appeared on each side of Jesus.

Why Moses and Elijah? The scriptural meaning of their presence is that Moses symbolizes the dead and the old law while Elijah symbolizes life and the prophecy.

We must remember that Moses received the old Law and when he died he was buried on Mount Moab. Elijah is the only prophet who did not die and went up to heaven on a chariot of fire.

So, they appeared with Jesus to show us (and the Apostles present) that Jesus was the fulfillment of the old Law and the prophets as the Messiah, and the voice of God confirmed all of this with His Words: "This is my Beloved Son, listen to Him."

Personal Significance:

The Church at the top of Mount Tabor is absolutely beautiful and captures the full sense of what happened on this site. When you look at this Church you will see a "cap" on top and, when I saw this, I pictured a direct 'ray of grace' from this chapel to heaven. I am sure that you can picture this also, as this ray of light has appeared in some movies.

Once inside this Church it confirmed my picture as it

is a dome Church and the mosaic of the Transfiguration is something that I will never forget, especially with God the Father at the very top.

Praying in this Church was a blessed moment and the words of St. Peter came to me..."Lord, it is good for us to be here!"

The magnificence of this place filled me with the realization that God the Father loves me so much that He sent His Son to live and die and rise to open the gates of heaven.

My task is to respond to the words of God the Father when He said, "This is My Beloved Son, listen to Him!"

Listening to Jesus to pick up my cross and follow Him, to love my enemies, to care for the sick and the poor, to love my neighbor as myself are all things for me that need grace. The grace of the Holy Spirit must fill my heart as I strive to become more aware of Jesus and His Will in my life.

The Transfiguration was a total change of Jesus and He is asking me for a total change. I don't know how long it will take to make a total change and I may not ever achieve it but I do know that I must keep trying to listen to Jesus...that is the only way.

I have a reminder on my desk of the Transfiguration. It is a rock from Mount Tabor which has multiple meanings. The rock of my faith, Jesus as the cornerstone, the place where the Transfiguration occurred, the place where one of the Apostles could have stood and more, if I pray about it.

Snippets (Lorrie):

It was an early morning call and the air was chill as I grabbed a shawl to take with me. We gathered as a group and got seated on our bus, two by two. Our guide explained that our tour bus was much too large to be able to make the hairpin, switchback turns on Mt. Tabor, so we would be transferring to smaller shuttle buses to make the journey up to the top.

I'm sure this trip to the top was every tour guides worst nightmare, as he tried hard to count and make sure that he had each of the pilgrims in our group accounted for. We were not the only large group headed to the top that morning.

Once at the top we walked to the church called The Church of the Transfiguration and listened outside as our guide gave us the story of what we call the "Transfiguration," when Jesus took Peter, James and John met Moses and Elijah and was transfigured in glory on that mountain top.

"his face did shine as the sun, and his garments became white as the light.

> *"And behold, there appeared unto them*
>   *Moses and Elijah talking with him."*

(Matthew 17:2-3)

Chapter 10
―――――――
"THE OUR FATHER" - JERUSALEM

"Pray, then, in this way: 'Our Father, who is in heaven..."Matthew 6: v9 thru 13

Geographic Significance:

Jerusalem both now and in the past is the central city for the faith of the Jewish nation. Jerusalem is where the major synagogues are located and the Great Temple.

It is a city with over 2000 years of history and there are parts of it that speak loud and clear about this history.

One might say that "all roads lead to Jerusalem" as there are direct roadways into and out of Jerusalem from many other cities such as Bethlehem, Galilee, Jericho, and others.

There is a hill where you can see the vastness of this city and this is where Jesus stopped to continue to teach His Apostles

∼

Scriptural Significance:

Of course, we all know that it was in Jerusalem that Jesus walked His final walk to Golgotha, where He was crucified. But there are also other times involving the presence of Jesus such as His presentation in the Temple (Bethlehem is not far from Jerusalem); talking with the Elders when He was twelve; going to Jerusalem with His parents (and later with His mother) on the feasts of Passover, Dedication, and Tabernacles; and of course, His last trip on Passover.

Jesus, on one of his journeys to Jerusalem, taught the people in various parts of the city. He was well known before He came to Jerusalem, so you can imagine what people did when they heard He was here.

Once, as they approached the city, Jesus stopped on this hilltop in order to look out over the city for the last time. It was here that His disciples asked Him how they should pray and He gave them (and us) the Our Father. It is a prayer of praise, forgiveness, obedience, dependence and trust.

Personal Significance:

Standing on the Mount of Olives and looking out over the city as Jesus did, gave me a chill.

Here, we visited the Church of the Pater Noster built on the traditional site where Jesus taught His Apostles the Lord's Prayer.

Knowing that it was from here the Jesus would begin His entrance into the city for the last time caused me to stop and picture His Apostles resting and talking among themselves, even looking at the face of Jesus and seeing something different about it. I can see myself looking into the face of Jesus and wondering what was on His mind and what could I do to help Him and share His thoughts.

It was (and is) a perfect time to ask Jesus to teach me how to pray. Now when I (and you) say this prayer, I say it slowly and focus on the greatness of this perfect prayer.

Jesus knows where each of us are in our prayer life and He helps us in this prayer to realize how much God (His Father) loves us. To say "Our Father…" I realize that we are all brothers and sisters in the Lord. Jesus did not say "My Father" but "Our Father" which makes Jesus my brother.

The beginning of this prayer teaches us that we are all one family striving to be closer to God and we can help each other on the way.

Next, we recognize where Our Father is and praise Him for His goodness…"who art in heaven, hallowed by Your name".

We then pray for His greatness to come to all of us as we say "Thy kingdom come" and as good children of God "Thy will be done on earth as it is in heaven".

When I say 'Thy will be done', I know that it means that I should recognize His place in my life and that I should do what I inwardly know is His will for me. I truly must pray for that since it sometimes is difficult to recognize His will in my life.

Next, I ask for the daily strength to do His will in my life and to become closer to Him with this strength.

"Give us this day, our daily bread..." does not only mean food for strength, but far more, in that it means the spiritual strength to live this day in God's presence.

This spiritual 'bread' can be my daily prayers, going to Mass and receiving Communion, reading Scripture, or any other way that we can recognize we will receive His grace during the day.

Now the action that definitely reminds us of the great gift our brother Jesus gave us when we say what he did..."forgiving us our trespasses (sins) as we forgive those who trespass against us". If I focus on this action during the day it truly makes me humble to receive this grace and to recognize the power of forgiveness and love in my life.

Now, I truly need His help, so I ask God, Our Father, to "lead us not into temptation but, deliver us from evil."

His grace and my recognition of how to use this grace (to stay away from temptation), helps me to avoid sin, and to be delivered from evil.

This is my prayer. This may not happen every time,

but picturing Jesus on this very hilltop and teaching me the power of this prayer makes me realize how much I am loved.

Hopefully when you say this prayer, you too, will realize how much "Our Father" loves you!

∽

Snippets (Lorrie):

The Lord's Prayer seems to be one of those universal prayers to which most people know every word.

It was in this spot on the Mount of Olives that He gave us this prayer. Our guide told us that Jesus was in a certain place praying, and when He had finished, one of His disciples said, "Lord, teach us to pray.

He said to them, "When you pray, this is what you say:

> *"Father, hallowed be Your name. Your kingdom come. Give us this day our daily bread. And forgive us our sins, For we ourselves forgive everyone indebted to us. And do not bring us to the time of trial."*

Taken from: Luke 11:1-4

It felt very special to be in the place where Jesus gave us this special prayer. Each time I say a decade of the rosary, I am reminded of time I spent on the Mount of Olives.

Chapter 11

"THE MOUNT OF OLIVES" - JERUSALEM

"When He approached Jerusalem, He saw the city and wept over it, saying, 'If you had known....'" Luke 19: v41-45

∼

Geographic Significance:

The Mount of Olives is on the western side of the city of Jerusalem. It has its name due to the tremendous number of olive trees that grow on this mountainside. In fact, this Mount was the place to get the oil (olive oil) to anoint the kings of Israel. It is also the point where the Jews light the first fire to declare the holy days.

It is located at the edge of the Judean Mountains and the Judean Desert can be seen off in the distance. It is a beautiful location outside of the city of Jerusalem and, at one time, had about 24 churches and monasteries.

Today, there are only about three that are left. Near the bottom of the Mount, one will find the Garden of Gethsemane which we will talk about later.

SCRIPTURAL SIGNIFICANCE:

The Mount of Olives has a number of great Scriptural events that happen at certain sections of this Mount.

As stated in Chapter Ten, part of this Mount is where Jesus taught the Our Father to the Apostles and where He looked out and wept for the people of Israel. The eastern slope of the Mount of Olives shows the humanity of Jesus when He weeps over Lazarus and the western slope shows the divinity of Jesus when He weeps over His own people and His dwelling place.

There is a church on the western side with the name "Dominus Flevit," which is Latin for 'The Master Wept'. He is God in the flesh and weeps while looking at the Temple and the fire of sacrifices coming out of the Holy of Holies, the dwelling place of God. He weeps because there is a separation going on. God is separating Himself from His own people, Israel.

The Mount of Olives is also stated to be the place where Jesus ascended into heaven forty days after His Resurrection.

∼

Personal Significance:

Being among the beautiful olive trees was a wonderful experience.

Walking down the pathway that Jesus took entering into the city of Jerusalem, with our pilgrim people, was another experience of the reminder of the crowd of people that were praising the entry of Jesus. The walking, the sharing with the other pilgrims, the view of the city of Jerusalem and the stopping at a spot overlooking the city were all moments of a historic memorial of time and a moment of grace where I had a true sense of being there.

In fact, I was looking around, both during the walk and at the spot where we stopped, for Jesus. Yes, it may sound strange but with all of the talk about the Mount of Olives and Jesus growing up...I tried to put it all together as an adult and received a 'religious' moment.

Not only is the Mount of Olives a true place of multiple memorials, I began to realize that it was from this point that Jesus would have realized what was ahead of Him.

I remembered the picture above the tabernacle in the church. It is the picture of Jesus with the crown of thorns, His Immaculate Heart and tears coming down His cheeks. The words on the bottom of the picture are "Sic Deus Dilexit Mundum" which means "For God So Loved The World". The full picture was imaged in my mind and all I could think about was the divine decision that God loved me so much and that His Son, Jesus, loved me so much that He followed His Father's will and gave up His life for me.

This was truly a moment of grace and I become 'filled' again each time I look at this picture.

SNIPPETS (LORRIE):

Our guide told us about how Jesus taught during the day, but at night he would come back to the Mount of Olives to hide.

He felt safe there because the mount was full of graves and the Jews didn't get close to the tombs and graves because it was considered a defiling act (according to the book of Leviticus and the Law of Moses).

Our guide went on to say. that there was a cave located at the top of the Mount of Olives where He was hiding and also teaching His disciples, especially the great prayer, Our Father In Heaven (Luke 11). And that after Constantine declared Christianity as the official religion of the whole Roman Empire in 325 A.D., his mother, Helen, came to the Holy Land and built a massive basilica on the top of the Mount of Olives...over the same cave where Jesus had been hiding every night and teaching His disciples. The basilica was called "the Eleona" which means 'the olive tree.' (A Spiritual Journey, Raed Mukhouli)

Chapter 12

"THE GARDEN OF GETHSEMANE" - JERUSALEM

"And He was saying, 'Abba! Father! All things are possible for You; remove this cup from Me; yet not what I will, but what you will." Mark 14: v36

Geographic Significance:

The Garden of Gethsemane is located at the base of the Mount of Olives. In this garden, the olive press for making olive oil was found. When the olives are ready to pick, it is much easier to pick the olives off the mountain and carry them downhill then it is to walk them uphill, hence the location of the olive press.

The garden itself has various trees within it and you see all of them as you walk through. I noticed that some of the trees/scrubs had branches that entangled each other and could easily have make a 'crown of thorns'.

From this location, it was a short walk to the actual city gate entrance.

~

SCRIPTURAL **S**IGNIFICANCE:

We all recognize the name "Garden of Gethsemane" as the place where Jesus went after the Last Supper and prayed.

In many photos, Jesus is kneeling at the side of a large stone and appears to be in torment. In fact, it is stated that Jesus was in such agony that His sweat was in the form of beads of blood.

In the garden, a church has been built. It is called the Church of All Nations, since after World War I, fourteen nations contributed money to build the church.

In front of the altar of this church is the 'Rock of the Agony' where the Lord Jesus knelt down on His knees and asked to have this 'cup' (His death) pass but that He would always follow the will of His Father.

It should also be noted that the word "Gethsemane" is taken from the Aramaic or the Hebrew and means 'olive press'. This is appropriate since it is located at the bottom of the Mount of Olives.

It is also appropriate since the four major uses of olive oil is for food; light; anointing/beauty and healing. Here, we can state that like the olive, Jesus is crushed and becomes our Food; He is also the Light of the world; as it says in Scripture, when we fast (during Lent especially) we should anoint our head with olive oil and with our Lord's suffering, we can quote the prophet Isaiah "By His wounds, we are healed!".

∽

Personal Significance:

Walking slowly through the Garden of Gethsemane brought many different thoughts:

Would I walk with Jesus all the way?

When He asked me to stop and pray while He went on further to pray, would I pray or fall asleep?

Since I know the outcome of the night and the next couple of days, how earnest in prayer would I be?

Would I mourn Jesus' death?

Would I be fearful that others would criticize me for sharing my faith loudly or be energetic about the death and Resurrection?

These thoughts went through my head as I walked through the garden, but when I went into the Church and knelt down in front of the Rock that Jesus knelt by, I couldn't help but feel totally exhausted.

Why, I don't know, but I felt exhausted and almost frozen in time. I prayed with my hand on the Rock and felt emotion flowing from me to the Rock and from the Rock to me. I could not get up! More people came in and I suddenly realized that I was blocking others who also wanted to pray. I got up and walked backwards away from the Rock. Jesus was in agony and I was leaving Him also…just as His Apostles did.

I knew at that point that I had to find a way in my life to get closer to Jesus and to never leave Him alone again. I wanted Him to always know how much I loved Him for giving up His life for me.

Snippets (Lorrie):

A rainy day greeted us as we gathered together to visit the Mount of Olives. We were warned that the climb up the road from the bus was steep and slippery and were given the choice to go with the group or remain below near the Garden.

I chose to stay below with a few others in the vicinity of the Garden of Gethesame. We stepped into the Garden area from the street and a walled fence to see a black wrought iron fence surrounding 12 or so very gnarled and misshapen olive trees. The fence was in place to keep the visitors from trampling the space.

The Garden had a lovely smell, consisting of rosemary, lavender and roses. Terra-cotta bowls along the pathways held pansy's of different colors.

I stood by the black fence with my field notebook and a pencil and sketched the Garden so that I could remember the memory. I took time here to rest and pray, while waiting for the others to return.

I particularly reflected on how many times I have wished that a certain difficult task or event might be taken away from me. In this way I connected personally with what happened in this very garden when Jesus prayed here and wept.

I felt a small quiet voice within saying to rest and take it all in so that I could learn not only to be patient" but to be more obedient to His will in my life. I held onto the cold and wet railing and let the tears drip down my cheek unchecked.

The group reappeared and we were led into the Church of All Nations, which is erected to the right of the Garden area. It was very stark inside and we made our way past the wooden pews to the front where many people were looking down at the floor at the front of the altar.

There was a railing around the outside of the rock. Our guide told us about the design of the doves affixed to the railing. The doves were bending their heads down and spreading their wings. This was a sign the dove does before it dies. It bows the head and spreads its wings and then drops dead. The dove here is to symbolize the last days of the Lord Jesus.

As I approached this space, I saw a very wide grey rock resting on the floor, actually, the church was constructed around that rock, as this was the actual rock where Jesus prayed in the Garden, just before he was betrayed. He knelt down on His knees and said, "Father, if possible, let this cup pass from Me, but let it be according to your will."

As I, myself, knelt down and put both of my hands on that rock and I prayed to be more like Him in my daily life and to grow closer to Him and live in HIs love - to be wholly His.

Looking up, with tears and a full heart, I gazed at the painting behind the altar where Jesus is depicted sitting on the rock with the dove hovering over His head and olive trees on both sides of the rock.

I stepped out the the darkened church into the light of the the day and noticed that I felt lighter and realized that a release had occurred deep within.

Chapter 13

THE UPPER ROOM

"Where is the guest room in which I may eat the Passover with My disciples?...He took some bread, blessed it, broke it and gave it to His disciples saying, 'This is My Body which will be given up for you'. In the same way, He took the cup saying 'Drink this all of you, This is the Cup of My blood of the new covenant which will be poured out for many for the forgiveness of sins'." Matthew 26, 26 thru 28

∼

Geographic Significance:

The Upper Room, where Jesus had the Last Supper,

was in Jerusalem on the second floor of an ordinary house. There was/is no fanfare about it. It is fairly large and has some beautiful scenes on the walls.

Our group fit in this room very comfortably along with another tour group. Without the scenes on the walls, it is a very plain and simple room and nothing really attractive about it.

Our tour guide talked about this room and how this simple, plain room was spirit-filled.

Scriptural Significance:

This Upper Room has significant scriptural presence and meaning in three distinct ways. First, it is the Room where the First Holy Eucharist took place. It is where Our Lord gave us this great sacrament and said, "Do this in memory of Me!"

It is where Jesus acknowledged His betrayer and then proceeded to wash His Apostles feet as well as share with us the beautiful analogy of the vine and the branches.

This is where, in John's Gospel, He tells His Apostles and us many things about His love for us and says a number of times 'love one another as I have loved you!'

The second significant moment in this room is that it is where Jesus came to His Apostles after He had risen from the dead. The Apostles were very frightened after the death of Jesus and did not know what to do. Jesus appeared to them and they were amazed and began to truly believe in Him. They learned more and more from Him each time He came to them.

The third significant moment in this room is when the Holy Spirit, on Pentecost, came to them and filled them with the fire of Divine Love. The Holy Spirit filled them in such a way that they not only believed in Jesus but also proclaimed Him to others loudly and compassionately. It is the day that they left the Upper Room filled with the strength of the Holy Spirit and preached all over Jerusalem. It is the day that Peter brought thousands into the faith.

∼

Personal Significance:

Initially walking into this room, I really did not have

any spiritual impact. I saw how plain it was and there was nothing attractive about it.

But as the tour guide began to talk about what happened in this room, I began to sense the power present.

If only walls could talk, they could tell me of the human presence of Jesus here and giving us His sacramental life forever. The walls could also tell me of the divine presence of Jesus and how His fulfillment of Scripture and His fulfillment of His own words gave strength to the Apostles. The walls could also tell me of the power of the Holy Spirit in giving the Apostles the words and actions to transform so many people on the day of Pentecost.

Looking around and trying to envision these moments of grace, I was startled and overcome in trying to take it all in. There was a stopping point within me that could only absorb so much and I know now that there was/is a lot more to absorb.

Today, as I think about this experience and the Upper Room, I pray that with each Eucharist and reception of Holy Communion, that I may receive the many graces coming from the Risen Christ and that the Holy Spirit may empower me to bring the message of

Salvation to everyone I meet. It is a memory that is ever present at each Eucharist.

SNIPPETS (LORRIE):

One by one our group of pilgrims climbed the stairs around the back of the building up into what is known as the Upper Room.

Personally, I had been looking forward to seeing this room because we had been in Milan and Rome recently and had seen the two famous versions of the Last Supper....so you can imagine my surprise and dismay to enter a large empty room!

This site is now owned and operated by the Israeli Department of the Interior and so it does not espouse any religious affiliation.

Now when you come to a situation such as this, you have two choices: 1. You can stay angry because it wasn't what you expected, or 2. You can close your eyes and envision what had been there according to what you heard and what you had read in the Bible.

Our guide was a religious catholic and was very well versed in ancient biblical history and he stood to one side, with our group gathered around, and the empty room started to come alive with the stories he told.

Some of the other holy sites had the ability to transport me back in time to the event that happened there, especially the tomb, because I was able to have a tangible item to touch.

In this case, I had only a room, my imagination and the biblical accounts written up about the Last Supper and the foot washing and the breaking of the bread and when Jesus reappeared and when the Holy Spirit filled the apostles with everything they needed to go forth.

That is quite a list of events that took place in this empty room.

I stood alone for a bit and tried to imagine where the table would have been placed...the table where they all sat together on Holy Thursday.

Did they run up the stairs in fear after the crucifixion, worried that the Roman soldiers were out looking for the followers of Jesus?

Did they wonder what they were supposed to do next? Or had they listened closely enough to Jesus when he was teaching and giving them the parables so that they would know what to do next?

I gazed at the thick stone walls and thought about Jesus coming through them and what their faces must have looked like when they realized that it was Him!

So many faith-filled experiences happened in this space. I stood apart from the group and prayed that I might be filled with faith and joy.

"Hurry, hurry," said our guide, he had more for us to see.

Chapter 14

"THE VIA DOLOROSA" - JERUSALEM

"So they cried out, 'Away with Him, away with Him, Crucify Him!' ...So he then handed Him over to them to be crucified. They took Jesus, therefore, and He went out, bearing His own cross, to the place called the Place of the Skull, which is called in Hebrew, Golgotha" John 19: v15 thru v17

Geographic Significance:

The Via Dolorosa is located in the old part of the city of Jerusalem and believed not to be cased in with a wall. The Via Dolorosa has many different interpreted names, the Way of the Cross; the Way of Sorrow; the Way of Suffering; the Painful Way; and the Walk of Sorrow. Most of us know it as the Way of the Cross, although, the Way of Sorrow is the best translation.

It is about a 2000 foot journey from the starting point (Antonio Fortress) to the foot of Golgotha. This distance may not appear far but think about doing it after being beaten for hours and then carrying a cross whose crossbar weighs at least 150 pounds.

The Via Dolorosa is not a straight path either; it bends around corners and zig zags here and there. This makes it much more difficult.

Today, the Via Dolorosa is bound by all different vendors...rugs salesmen, clothes sales, trinkets, vases, paintings, food, etc. It is a clumsy walk on cobblestone making each step somewhat dangerous.

∽

SCRIPTURAL SIGNIFICANCE:

The Via Dolorosa has an actual starting point since we believe that it begins where Jesus receives His cross at the Antonia Fortress. The Antonia Fortress overlooks the Temple and was the headquarters of the Roman ruler in Israel. Here, after the horrendous scourging and crowning of thorns is where Pilate makes the final decision to crucify Jesus on a cross.

This journey along the Via Dolorosa is one of various statements in Scripture and various traditional stories involved with our faith.

Walking along the route and recognizing the many places where the believers of our past state that certain actions took place, helps one to focus on the specific journey rather then the distractions of the vendors.

Stopping and praying at spots where Our Lord fell should allow us to recall the past or current physical pains in our lives that, offered to Jesus, can be graced with His help.

Focusing on the journey and Scripture, we can receive many graces as we pray for the awareness of Simon in recognizing how we can carry our cross with Jesus by our side.

In helping someone with a physical need, we can remember Veronica who wiped the sweat and blood from Jesus' face and who was given the grace of His presence planted not only on the cloth but also in her heart.

Each station along the Via Dolorosa is an experience of the presence of Jesus in our lives as we walk our own 'way of the cross.

∽

Personal Significance:

As you can begin to perceive, walking the Via Dolorosa, today, requires focus in finding each Station Marker.

Along with our own pilgrims, there were other pilgrims praying in different languages and carrying crosses. There were many distractions, which is why I needed to focus. I was initially distracted by many different things...people pushing, people speaking different languages, people singing, vendors shouting, etc.

I think that it was after the third station that I realized how distracted I was and I forced myself to focus on Jesus and asked Him to help me. With that, I began to realize how distracted my life is on a daily basis in trying to follow Jesus. It was like I was in a protected bubble looking out and seeing all of these activities as distractions to my faith. Not only the activities going on around me on the Via, but also the distracting activities of the daily life like people asking me to do something that keeps me from prayer or church or daily TV/radio that takes away from prayer time or even special time with my family.

As I do the stations now, I can remember this somewhat distracting time and my memory helps me to focus on the station itself and Jesus, as well as, how much I am loved by God that He would send His Son to die for me.

The actual Via Dolorosa consists of Station One – *Jesus sentenced to die on the Cross* - through Station Nine – *Jesus falling for the Third Time*; the final five Stations are in the Church of the Holy Sepulcher. So, as we reached this Church, where we were to celebrate Mass, I recognized the final steps to the Crucifixion were to be prayed as a community.

I prayed that beginning with the stripping of Jesus of His clothes, I and we as a community would strip ourselves of those things that keep us from knowing the Lord more closely. Also, I would strive to listen more intently to the final words of Jesus from the Cross.

SNIPPETS (LORRIE):

Today was the day when we would walk the Way of the Cross and visit the site where Jesus was crucified and we would get to see the tomb.

I made sure I took my knee medicine and rubbed both knees with arnica from a fellow pilgrim. I knew deep within that this day would be hard – not only physically, but also spiritually and emotionally.

The bus dropped off our group on a side street outside of the old city. We walk through a short cut, to the other side of the walled area, and come through St. Stephen's Gate.

Once inside, the walkway between the shops was very narrow and made of uneven rocks with occasional steps that went up and down. You really had to focus so that you didn't get lost, to keep your footing, all the while being jostled, and being curious about all the shops that lined either side of the walkway.

I saw women doing their weekly grocery shopping in these shops, purchasing orange lentils and olives, while others were in up-to-date camera shops purchasing cards for their digital cameras. It was a place where the old and the new clashed happily together.

The sights, sounds and smells were loud and chaotic, with many different languages being spoken around us. Shoppers were haggling with shopkeepers in the small shops set on either side of the walkway. Men sat in chairs at the front of their shops smoking pungent cigarettes and cigars that wafted through the confined space.

I was very aware of the noise, the close quarters and the confusion and the noise as we navigated the walkways that had twisting turns and we were told again and again to stay with the group. I could see a hand go up by one of our pilgrims letting those of us further back know that the group was getting ready to make a left or right turn up ahead. (I think they may have been worried that someone - like me - might get separated and lost during this portion of our pilgrimage. I had been lost once, and I did not want it to happen again!)

It was surprising to me then, that we gathered together along the walkway and our guide held up his hand up above his head and pointed to the first station of the cross. People were walking past, our group intent on their own shopping or sightseeing.

Note: look closely at the cover and see what I mean - this is one of the stations of the cross.

I tried to imagine in my mind's eye what this might have been like when Christ walked it while carrying his cross. Of course I have seen numerous movies depicting him doing this very act - the most recent in my mind was the movie, "The Passion of Christ." I wondered what it would have been like to rent a cross and attempt to carry it along this same walkway?

We continued to hurry along, again worried about time, since we had a guaranteed time in the Church of the Holy Sepulcher for a mass for our group. We stepped off the pathway into a walled garden area and from there walked into the Church.

Chapter 15

"THE CRUCIFIXION AND HOLY SEPULCHRE: - JERUSALEM

"Father, forgive them for they know not what they are doing?...And Jesus crying out in a loud voice: Father, into Your hands I commit My Spirit."..... But on the first day of the week, at early dawn, they came to the tomb bringing the spices, which they had prepared. And they found the stone rolled away from the tomb, but when they entered, they did not find the body of the Lord. " Luke 24: vi...v3

Geographic Significance:

The site of Calvary has been marked by a Church since 335 A.D. While it is now well within the walls of Jerusalem's Old City, in the time of Jesus, it was a small hill just outside the western walls and there certainly could have been a garden there.

Also, it has been believed that Jesus was not only crucified on the top of this hill but that He was also buried in the tomb of Joseph of Arimathea at the bottom of this hill.

Therefore, Jesus rose from this same location. Significant to our faith about this location is that we, as a historical Church, note that for 300 years the early Christians accepted this location and prayed there in memory of these moments of faith.

Scriptural Significance:

The Scriptural significance starts with Station Ten – the stripping of Jesus' clothes – in the fact that Jesus was at the final spot of His Crucifixion.

The rest of the Stations – Eleven through Fourteen – are all actions that occur at Golgotha.

After the death of Jesus, the burial of Jesus is found inside the Holy Sepulcher Church – the tomb.

Inside this Church, to experience the place where Jesus died, buried and rose from the dead is located (and protected) in a very small space below a beautiful altar. One must get on the floor in front of this altar and reach into the spot to place your hand on this spot believing that you have, indeed, been involved with a faith moment and that moment has changed lives.

To be in this Church and complete the Stations is a beautiful and sacred experience. As an aside, when Constantine declared the Holy Roman Empire in 325 A.D., he sent emissaries to Jerusalem to find the empty tomb of Jesus. Eusebius of Cesarea discovered Golgotha and the empty tomb and people built the Church (335 A.D. see above).

Queen Helen (the mother of Constantine), was so excited, she wanted to find the cross of Jesus. She spent many years looking and was in despair until someone told her that there was a man named Judah who knew where the cross was. After much pressure, he took them to a water cistern full of rubble, soil, stones and rocks. There they discovered the nails, the hammer and three crosses.

She did not know which cross was the cross of Jesus but, as it may, a funeral was passing by and she stopped the funeral and placed one of the crosses on the coffin but nothing happened. She then placed the second cross on the coffin and again, nothing happened. But when she placed the third cross on the coffin, the young dead man came alive and started to knock on the coffin. By this miracle, she knew that this was the Cross of Christ. She protected this cross and brought it to the Church of the Holy Sepulcher.

Pieces of this Sacred Cross has been separated and brought to many different parts of the world.

∼

Personal Significance:

Needless to say, the last five Stations that are located inside the Church are beautiful moments to experience.

Although it was very crowded, focus was truly required. Since our pilgrimage was scheduled to celebrate Mass in this Church, the time was strictly monitored so we would not lose our place.

There were stairs and steps throughout our walk and

my spirit was feeling the wonderful gift of the presence of Jesus, especially the closer I got to the "spot" designated as the point of His Death, burial and Resurrection. I remember being with Lorrie in the line and moving slowly closer. The time became a pressure for me as I was going to be Deacon at our Mass. So I focused and looked around at the 'sites' in the Church.

Looking around and thinking of Jesus being stripped of His garments and being thrown down on the cross brought water to my eyes. Focusing on His strength while hanging on this cross gave me the message of how strong I must be in bearing my crosses in life. Not just physical pain but also emotional and spiritual pain among the various daily calls for service. His words...forgive them; I thirst; you will be with Me in heaven; abandonment; behold your Mother; it is finished...all rang in my ears as I walked slowly to the "spot". As I reached this magnificent altar, I knelt down and looked into the space and saw the "designated spot". My heart fluttered, and I felt pressure actually looking at the spot. I reached in and placed my hand on the spot and felt tears building in my eyes and then my heart soared as I realized the magnificence of where I was. The death and Resurrection of my Savior, Jesus. As I got up and moved along, I realized how special this trip has been and looked forward to celebrating Mass.

Mass at the Church of the Holy Sepulcher was very special. Our pilgrimage people were actually joined by a "vagabond" who came in and sat in the back of the chapel. He did not cause any mischief during Mass as we (the celebrants and I) looked out; in fact, during the Sign of Peace, he went around and gave EVERYONE a handshake as the sign of peace. I thought that he was actually our "Jesus" attending our final Eucharistic celebration. For me, he was my reminder of how Jesus wants us to treat everyone, whether we know them or not. He did not cause any trouble and thanked us for allowing him to celebrate with us. Truly a gift from God!

I can't wait to go back again!!!!!!!!

Snippets (Lorrie):

This church was built over the site of Golgotha, where Christ was crucified. Again, in my minds eye I saw those 3 crosses in the distance up on a hill. Today that original site is thought to be inside this church.

I followed the others up the stairs and waited in line

to approach the altar and then got down on my knees so I could reach back under the altar to touch the star on the floor where they believe the crucifixion took place. I bent down and kissed this spot and silently expressed my thanks to our Lord for what He was willing to do for our sakes.

It's hard to imagine how emotional this act was for most of the pilgrims - the ability to physically be at the spot where Christ was crucified and to touch it, take it in and understand it in a way that I had previously been unable to do. It was one of the most memorable moments of the entire trip.

We walked through the winding halls within the church to a small chapel where our group assembled for mass. It was such a wonderful opportunity to celebrate the remembrance of what our Lord did for us and to receive the Eucharist in memory of HIm.

We filed out of the chapel and made our way to the Edicule - which is a box-like structure placed in the center of a large hall. The empty tomb is contain within this structure.

Our group lined up, five abreast and inched our way toward the tomb. My knees were really aching and there were no seats to take the pressure off of them.

I tried to remember how difficult it had been for Christ and if he could bear all of that for me - what was a little knee pain? I did not want to go home and have any regrets about not having seen or touched the places that were so important in my faith. With both hands I touched the empty tomb and thus ended our pilgrimage to the Holy Land - truly a trip of a lifetime where we were able to touch our faith with each step we took.

www.ingramcontent.com/pod-product-compliance
Lightning Source LLC
Chambersburg PA
CBHW060336050426
42449CB00011B/2773